OCT   1994

Deadly Sins

THOMAS PYNCHON

Deadly

MARY GORDON

JOHN UPDIKE

WILLIAM TREVOR

Illustrations by Etienne Delessert

GORE VIDAL

Sins

RICHARD HOWARD

A. S. BYATT

JOYCE CAROL OATES

William Morrow and Company, Inc.
New York

241.3
D

These essays originally appeared in *The New York Times Book Review.*
Used by permission.

Copyright © 1993
Thomas Pynchon　Gore Vidal
Mary Gordon　Richard Howard
John Updike　A. S. Byatt
William Trevor　The Ontario Review, Inc.

Illustrations copyright © 1993 by Etienne Delessert

All rights reserved. No part of this book may be reproduced or utilized in any form or by any means, electronic or mechanical, including photocopying, recording, or by any information storage or retrieval system, without permission in writing from the Publisher. Inquiries should be addressed to Permissions Department, William Morrow and Company, Inc., 1350 Avenue of the Americas, New York, N.Y. 10019.

It is the policy of William Morrow and Company, Inc., and its imprints and affiliates, recognizing the importance of preserving what has been written, to print the books we publish on acid-free paper, and we exert our best efforts to that end.

Library of Congress Cataloging-in-Publication Data

Deadly sins / Thomas Pynchon . . . [et al.] ; illustrations by Etienne Delessert.
p. cm.
Essays originally published in *The New York Times Book Review.*
ISBN 0-688-13690-7
1. Deadly sins. I. Pynchon, Thomas.
BV4626.D43 1994 94-9135
241'.3—dc20 CIP

Printed in the United States of America

First Edition

1 2 3 4 5 6 7 8 9 10

BOOK DESIGN BY RITA MARSHALL

Contents

Sloth   THOMAS PYNCHON   10

Anger   MARY GORDON   24

Lust   JOHN UPDIKE   40

Gluttony   WILLIAM TREVOR   52

Pride   GORE VIDAL   64

Avarice   RICHARD HOWARD   74

Envy   A. S. BYATT   82

Despair   JOYCE CAROL OATES   104

Deadly Sins

These seven essays and one poem first appeared serially in THE NEW YORK TIMES BOOK REVIEW during the summer of 1993. In introducing the series, the BOOK REVIEW editors said:

Three decades ago, Ian Fleming, while at THE SUNDAY TIMES OF LONDON, asked seven British writers—W. H. Auden, Cyril Connolly, Patrick Leigh Fermor, Edith Sitwell, Christopher Sykes, Evelyn Waugh, and Angus Wilson—to write about the deadly sins. Their essays were later published as THE SEVEN DEADLY SINS (Quill/Morrow). We, being envious of the idea, invited eight devilishly clever writers to choose their favorite transgression and go at it.

Yes, we know that eight is too many for seven sins. But when one writer wanted to write not about a deadly sin but about the one unforgivable sin of despair, we agreed, knowing that we would be forgiven.

Sloth

THOMAS
PYNCHON

IN

his classical discussion of the subject in the SUMMA THEOLOGICA, Aquinas termed Sloth, or *acedia*, one of the seven capital sins. He said he was using "capital" to mean "primary" or "at the head of" because such sins gave rise to others, but there was an additional and darker sense resonating luridly just beneath and not hurting the power of his argument, for the word also meant "deserving of capital punishment." Hence the equivalent term "mortal," as well as the punchier English "deadly."

But come on, isn't that kind of extreme, death for something as lightweight as Sloth? Sitting there on some medieval death row, going, "So, look, no offense, but what'd they pop you for anyway?"

"Ah, usual story, they came around at the wrong time of day, I end up taking out half of some sheriff's unit with my two-cubit crossbow, firing three-quarter-inch bolts on auto feed. Anger, I guess. . . . How about you?"

"Um, well . . . it wasn't anger. . . ."

"Ha! Another one of these Sloth cases, right?"

" . . . fact, it wasn't even me."

"Never is, slugger—say, look, it's almost time for lunch. You wouldn't happen to be a writer, by any chance?"

Writers of course are considered the mavens of Sloth. They are approached all the time on the subject, not only for free advice, but also to speak at Sloth Symposia, head up Sloth Task Forces, testify as expert witnesses at Sloth Hearings. The stereotype arises in part from our conspicuous presence in jobs where pay is by the word, and deadlines are tight and final—we are presumed to know from piecework and the convertibility of time and money. In addition, there is all the glamorous folklore surrounding writer's block, an affliction known sometimes to resolve itself dramatically and without warning, much like constipation, and (hence?) finding wide sympathy among readers.

Writer's block, however, is a trip to the theme park of your choice alongside the mortal sin that produces it. Like each of the other six, Sloth was supposed to be the progenitor of a whole family of lesser, or venial, sins, among them Idleness, Drowsiness, Restlessness of the Body, Instability, and Loquacity. "Acedia" in Latin means sorrow, deliberately self-directed, turned away from God, a loss of spiritual determination that then feeds back on in to the process, soon enough producing what are currently known as guilt and depression, eventually pushing us to where we will do anything, in the way of venial sin and bad judgment, to avoid the discomfort.

But Sloth's offspring, though bad—to paraphrase the Shangri-Las—
are not always evil, for example what Aquinas terms Uneasiness of the
Mind, or "rushing after various things without rhyme or reason," which,
"if it pertains to the imaginative power . . . is called curiosity." It is of
course precisely in such episodes of mental traveling that writers are
known to do good work, sometimes even their best, solving formal
problems, getting advice from Beyond, having hypnagogic adventures
that with luck can be recovered later on. Idle dreaming is often of the
essence of what we do. We sell our dreams. So real money actually
proceeds from Sloth, although this transformation is said to be even
more amazing elsewhere in the entertainment sector, where idle exercises
in poolside loquacity have not infrequently generated tens of millions
of dollars in revenue.

As a topic for fiction, Sloth over the next few centuries after Aquinas
had a few big successes, notably HAMLET, but not until arriving on the
shores of America did it take the next important step in its evolution.
Between Franklin's hectic aphorist, Poor Richard, and Melville's
doomed scrivener, Bartleby, lies about a century of early America, con-
solidating itself as a Christian capitalist state, even as acedia was in the
last stages of its shift over from a spiritual to a secular condition.

Philadelphia, by Franklin's time, answered less and less to the religious vision that William Penn had started off with. The city was becoming a kind of high-output machine, materials and labor going in, goods and services coming out, traffic inside flowing briskly about a grid of regular city blocks. The urban mazework of London, leading into ambiguities and indeed evils, was here all rectified, orthogonal. (Dickens, visiting in 1842, remarked, "After walking about in it for an hour or two, I felt that I would have given the world for a crooked street.") Spiritual matters were not quite as immediate as material ones, like productivity. Sloth was no longer so much a sin against God or spiritual good as against a particular sort of time, uniform, one-way, in general not reversible—that is, against clock time, which got everybody early to bed and early to rise.

Poor Richard was not shy in expressing his distaste for Sloth. When he was not merely repeating well-known British proverbs on the subject, he was contributing Great Awakening–style outbursts of his own—"O Lazy-bones! Dost think God would have given thee arms and legs if he had not designed thou shouldst use them?" Beneath the rubato of the day abided a stern pulse beating on, ineluctable, unforgiving, whereby whatever was evaded or put off now had to be made up for later, and at a higher level of intensity. "You may delay, but time will not." And Sloth, being continual evasion, just kept piling up like a budget deficit, while the dimensions of the inevitable payback grew ever less merciful.

In the idea of time that had begun to rule city life in Poor Richard's day, where every second was of equal length and irrevocable, not much in the course of its flow could have been called nonlinear, unless you counted the ungovernable warp of dreams, for which Poor Richard had scant use. In Frances M. Barbour's 1974 concordance of the sayings, there is nothing to be found under "Dreams," dreams being as unwelcome in Philly back then as their frequent companion, sleep, which was considered time away from accumulating wealth, time that had to be tithed back into the order of things to purchase twenty hours of productive waking. During the Poor Richard years, Franklin, according to the "Autobiography," was allowing himself from 1 A.M. to 5 A.M. for sleep. The other major nonwork block of time was four hours, 9 P.M. to 1 A.M., devoted to the Evening Question, "What good have I done this day?" This must have been the schedule's only occasion for drifting into reverie—there would seem to have been no other room for speculations, dreams, fantasies, fiction. Life in that orthogonal machine was supposed to be nonfiction.

By the time of BARTLEBY THE SCRIVENER: A STORY OF WALL-STREET (1853), acedia had lost the last of its religious reverberations and was now an offense against the economy. Right in the heart of robber-baron capitalism, the title character develops what proves to be terminal acedia. It is like one of those western tales where the desperado keeps making choices that only herd him closer to the one disagreeable finale. Bartleby just sits there in an office on Wall Street repeating, "I would prefer not to." While his options go rapidly narrowing, his employer, a man of affairs and substance, is actually brought to question the assumptions of his own life by this miserable scrivener—this writer!—who, though among the lowest of the low in the bilges of capitalism, nevertheless refuses to go on interacting anymore with the daily order, thus bringing up the interesting question: who is more guilty of Sloth, a person who collaborates with the root of all evil, accepting things-as-they-are in return for a paycheck and a hassle-free life, or one who does nothing, finally, but persist in sorrow? BARTLEBY is the first great epic of modern Sloth, presently to be followed by work from the likes of Kafka, Hemingway, Proust, Sartre, Musil, and others—take your own favorite list of writers after Melville and you're bound sooner or later to run into a character bearing a sorrow recognizable as peculiarly of our own time.

In this century we have come to think of Sloth as primarily political, a failure of public will allowing the introduction of evil policies and the rise of evil regimes, the worldwide fascist ascendancy of the 1920's and 30's being perhaps Sloth's finest hour, though the Vietnam era and the Reagan–Bush years are not far behind. Fiction and nonfiction alike are full of characters who fail to do what they should because of the effort involved. How can we not recognize our world? Occasions for choosing good present themselves in public and private for us every day, and we pass them by. Acedia is the vernacular of everyday moral life. Though it has never lost its deepest notes of mortal anxiety, it never gets as painful as outright despair, or as real, for it is despair bought at a discount price, a deliberate turning against faith in anything because of the inconvenience faith presents to the pursuit of quotidian lusts, angers, and the rest. The compulsive pessimist's last defense—

stay still enough and the blade of the scythe, somehow, will pass by—Sloth is our background radiation, our easy-listening station—it is everywhere, and no longer noticed.

Any discussion of Sloth in the present day is of course incomplete without considering television, with its gifts of paralysis, along with its creature and symbiont, the notorious Couch Potato. Tales spun in idleness find us Tubeside, supine, chiropractic fodder, sucking it all in, reenacting in reverse the transaction between dream and revenue that brought these colored shadows here to begin with so that we might feed, uncritically, committing the six other deadly sins in parallel, eating too much, envying the celebrated, coveting merchandise, lusting after images, angry at the news, perversely proud of whatever distance we may enjoy between our couches and what appears on the screen.

Sad but true. Yet, chiefly owing to the timely invention—not a minute too soon!—of the remote control and the VCR, maybe there is hope after all. Television time is no longer the linear and uniform commodity it once was. Not when you have instant channel selection, fast-forward, rewind, and so forth. Video time can be reshaped at will. What may have seemed under the old dispensation like time wasted and unrecoverable is now perhaps not quite as simply structured. If

Sloth can be defined as the pretense, in the tradition of American settlement and spoliation, that time is one more nonfinite resource, there to be exploited forever, then we may for now at least have found the illusion, the effect, of controlling, reversing, slowing, speeding, and repeating time—even imagining that we can escape it. Sins against video time will have to be radically redefined.

Is some kind of change already in the offing? A recent issue of THE NATIONAL ENQUIRER announced the winner of their contest for the King of Spuds, or top Couch Potato in the United States, culled from about a thousand entries. " 'All I do is watch television and work,' admits the 35-year-old bachelor, who keeps three TV sets blaring 24 hours a day at his Fridley, Minn., home and watches a fourth set on the job.

" 'There's nothing I like more than sitting around with a six-pack of beer, some chips and a remote control. . . . The TV station even featured me in a town parade. They went into my house, got my couch and put it on a float. I sat on the couch in my bathrobe and rode in the parade!' "

Sure, but is it Sloth? The fourth television set at work, the fact that twice, the Tuber in question mentions sitting and not reclining, suggest something different here. Channel-surfing and VCR-jockeying may require a more nonlinear awareness than may be entirely compatible with the venerable sin of Sloth—some inner alertness or tension, as of someone sitting in a yoga posture, or in Zen meditation. Is Sloth once more about to be, somehow, transcended? Another possibility of course is that we have not passed beyond acedia at all, but that it has only retreated from its long-familiar venue, television, and is seeking other, more shadowy environments—who knows? computer games, cult religions, obscure trading floors in faraway cities—ready to pop up again in some new form to offer us cosmic despair on the cheap.

Unless the state of our souls becomes once more a subject of serious concern, there is little question that Sloth will continue to evolve away from its origins in the long-ago age of faith and miracle, when daily life really was the Holy Ghost visibly at work and time was a story, with a beginning, middle, and end. Belief was intense, engagement deep and fatal. The Christian God was near. Felt. Sloth—defiant sorrow in the face of God's good intentions—was a deadly sin.

Perhaps the future of Sloth will lie in sinning against what now seems increasingly to define us—technology. Persisting in Luddite sorrow, despite technology's good intentions, there we'll sit with our heads in virtual reality, glumly refusing to be absorbed in its idle, disposable fantasies, even those about superheroes of Sloth back in Sloth's good old days, full of leisurely but lethal misadventures with the ruthless villains of the Acedia Squad.

Anger

MARY
GORDON

THERE

would be no point to sin if it were not the corridor to pleasure, but the corridor of anger has a particularly seductive, self-deceiving twist. More than any of the other sins, anger can be seen to be good, can perhaps even begin by being good. Jesus himself was angry, brandishing his whip and thrillingly overturning tables: coins, doves flying, the villainous sharpsters on their knees to save their spoils. It would seem to run in the family; by far the angriest character in the Old Testament is God.

Of all the sins, only anger is connected in the common tongue to its twinned, entwined virtue: justice. "Just anger," we say. Impossible even to begin to imagine such a phrase made with the others: try as you will, you can't get your mouth around the words "just sloth," or "just covetousness," to say nothing of the deadly breakfast cereal that sticks to the ribs for all eternity, "just lust."

Anger is electric, exhilarating. The angry person knows without a doubt he is alive. And the state of unaliveness, of partial aliveness, is so frequent and so frightening, the condition of inertia common, almost, as dirt, that there's no wonder anger feels like treasure. It goes through the body like a jet of freezing water; it fills the veins with purpose; it alerts the lazy eye and ear; the sluggish limbs cry out for movement; the torpid lungs grow rich with easy breath. Anger flows through the entire body, stem to stern, but its source and center is the mouth.

Its taste draws from those flavors that appeal to the mature and refined palate: the mix of sour, bitter, sweet, and salt, and something else, something slightly frightening, something chemical or at least inorganic, something unhealthful, something we suspect should not be there, a taste that challenges us because it might be poison—but if not, think what we have been able to withstand, then crave. Gin and Campari, the vinegary mint sauce alongside the Easter lamb, a grapefruit ice to cleanse the palate between heavy courses, a salad of arugula and cress, the salt around the margarita glass, all of them seeming to promise wisdom and a harsh, ascetic health.

The joy of anger is the joy—unforgettable from childhood—of biting down on a loose tooth. The little thorn (our own!) pressing into the tender pinkness of the gum, the labial exploration, the roughness we could impose on the thick and foolish tongue (a punishment for the times it failed us by refusing to produce the proper word?), and the delicious wince when we had gone too far. The mouth as self-contained, containing oracle. The truth: pain is possible. The freedom:

I can both inflict and endure. The harsh athletic contest, ultimately satisfying because of the alarming and yet deeply reassuring taste of blood.

Even the ancillary words, the names of anger's sidekicks, are a pleasure on the tongue. Spite, vengeance, rage. Just listen to the snaky "s," the acidic, arrowlike soft "g," the lucid, plosive "t" preceded by the chilled long "i," then dropped. The onomatopoeia of drawn swords. Nothing muffled, muffling, nothing concealing, nothing to protect the weak. To live in anger is to forget that one was ever weak, to believe that what others call weakness is a sham, a feint that one exposes and removes, like the sanitizing immolation of a plague-ridden house. The cruelty essential for the nation's greater health, because, after all, the weak pull down the strong. The angry one is radiant in strength, and, blazing like the angel with the flaming sword, banishes the transgressors from the garden they would only now defile.

Deadly anger is a hunger, an appetite that can grow like a glutton's or a lion's, seeking whom it may devour. Once fed, the creature grows hypnotized by itself. The brilliant Ford Madox Ford created an unforgettable character almost entirely moved by anger, Sylvia Tietjens, the beautiful, sadistic wife of the hero of his tetralogy, PARADE'S END.

Sylvia's mother explains her daughter's rage by using herself as an example: "I tell you I've walked behind a man's back and nearly screamed because of the desire to put my nails into the veins of his neck. It was a fascination."

This fascination begins in the mouth, then travels to the blood, thence to the mind, where it creates a connoisseur. One begins to note the intricate workmanship of one's own anger and soon to worship it, to devote oneself to its preservation, like any great work of art. Simple anger, the shallow, unaddictive kind, starts with a single action, and calls forth a single and finite response. You have done this to me, I will do that to you. An eye for an eye and a tooth for a tooth. In this bargain, there is hope for an end: eventually there will be no more eyes or teeth. But deadly anger is infinite; its whorls, emanating from themselves, grow ever smaller, but there is no end to the possibility of inward turning, inward fecundation.

Deadly anger is fanatic of embellishment. The angry person, like a Renaissance prince with endless coffers, travels the world in search of the right gem, the most exquisitely tinted snatch of silk, the perfect quarter-inch of ivory, the most incandescent golden thread, the feathers of the rara avis. The original cause of anger, like the base metal below the ornament, may long have been obscured by the fantastic encrustation. Even the plain desire to hurt may be lost in the detail of the justification for the hurting or the elaborations of the punishment. Anger takes on a life of its own, or it divorces itself from life in the service of death dealing, or life denying, or the compulsion to make someone's life unendurable simply for the sake of doing it, simply because it has become the shape of the angry one's life to punish.

The habit of punishment is quickly acquired and self-supporting. It has one food, plentiful and easily obtained: the need for blame. In this, it is a really very comprehensible attempt to render a senseless universe sensible. Everything that is, particularly everything that one wishes were otherwise, must have its cause, and so its causer. Perhaps the person taken over by deadly anger is for this reason, at bottom, pitiable, like Dostoyevsky's Grand Inquisitor, who demanded death on a large scale so that suffering could be reduced. We destroyed the village in order to save it. I destroy you because all that is wrong must be your fault. Accident is a concept of the weak-minded: what is wrong is someone's fault. Yours. And I must punish you. Furthermore, I demand that you see the rightness of your punishment.

This is the difference between the good, the necessary anger, the enlivening anger, and the deadly kind. The first is tied to justice, the death-dealing kind to punishment. This is the reason that the Greeks, who assumed their gods to be irrational, killing men like flies for their sport, wrote about anger so differently from the writers of the Old Testament, who assumed God to be a partner in their covenant. Saul's irrational and jealous rage, prompting him to seek David's death, is punished by the Lord. Moses' higher rage, causing the Levites to murder thousands of the children of Israel who had worshiped the golden calf, was prompted by their violation of the law. But Achilles, dragging the corpse of Hector around the walls of Troy, was acting from no impulse of justice or law. Only from an insistence upon mastery, upon a display of power, which makes a defiled thing of its object. Thinking it is fixed on its object, deadly anger actually forgets him, and is carried up in the black cloud of its own dominion. The country of deadly anger, with its own cultures, its own laws. A country ruled by a tyrant so obsessed with the fulfillment of his desire that all else is lost.

I am reminded of a story the Polish writer Ryszard Kapuscinski told me once about Idi Amin. Amin ordered, as he often did, one of his ministers to be summarily executed. The man was hanged. The next day, Amin said: "And where is my friend the minister, who is so amusing? Bring him here, I wish to see him." When he was told the man had been executed, he ordered the execution of those who had complied with his original orders.

Anger, in feeding on itself, creates around itself the overfed flesh of limitless indulgence. At the same time it emanates a styptic breath that withers hope and youth and beauty. So the angry person is at once two creatures: gross and bestial in the fulfillment of his appetites, desiccated, fleshless, nearly skeletal with the effort to keep active the tiny coal that fuels his passion.

If the word "sin" has any useful meaning at all in a time when there is no possibility of redemption, it must speak about a distortion so severe that the recognizable self is blotted out or lost. Many current thinkers wish to abandon the idea of a continuous self; novelists have always known that selves are fleeting, malleable, porous. Nevertheless some recognizable thing, something constant enough to have a name sensibly fixed to it, seems to endure from birth to death. Sin makes the sinner unrecognizable.

I experienced this once myself, and I remember it because it frightened me. I became an animal. This sinful experience occurred—as so many do—around the occasion of a dinner party. It was a hot August afternoon. I was having ten people for dinner that evening. No one was giving me a bit of help. I was, of course, feeling like a victim, as everyone does in a hot kitchen on an August day. (It is important to remember that the angry person's habit of self-justification is often connected to his habit of seeing himself as a victim.) I had been chopping, stirring, bending over a low flame, and all alone, alone! The oven's heat was my purgatory, my crucible.

My mother and my children thought this was a good time for civil disobedience. They positioned themselves in the car and refused to move until I took them swimming. Now my children were at tender ages at that time, seven and four. My mother was seventy-eight and, except for her daily habit of verbal iron-pumping, properly described as infirm. They leaned on the horn and shouted my name out the window, well within hearing of the neighbors, reminding me of my promise to take them to the pond.

There are certain times when a popular cliché disgorges itself from the dulled setting of overuse and comes to life, and this was one of them. I lost it. I lost myself. I jumped on the hood of the car. I pounded on the windshield. I told my mother and my children that I was never, ever going to take any of them anywhere and none of them were ever going to have one friend in any house of mine until the hour of their death, which, I said, I hoped was soon. I couldn't stop pounding on the windshield. Then the frightening thing happened. I became a huge bird. A carrion crow. My legs became hard stalks; my eyes were sharp and vicious. I developed a murderous beak. Greasy black feathers took the place of arms. I flapped and flapped. I blotted out the sun's light with my flapping. Each time my beak landed near my victims (it seemed to be my fists on the windshield, but it was really my beak on their necks) I went back for more. The taste of blood entranced me. I wanted to peck and peck forever. I wanted to carry them all off in my bloody beak and drop them on a rock where I would feed on their battered corpses till my bird stomach swelled.

I don't mean this figuratively: I became that bird. I had to be forced to get off the car and stop pounding the windshield. Even then I didn't come back to myself. When I did, I was appalled. I realized I had genuinely frightened my children. Mostly because they could no longer recognize me. My son said to me: "I was scared because I didn't know who you were."

I understand that this is not a sin of a serious nature. I know this to be true because it has its comic aspects, and deadly sin is characterized by the absence of humor, which always brings life. But because of that experience and others I won't tell you about, I understand the deadly sin of anger. I was unrecognizable to myself and, for a time, to my son, but I think I still would have been recognizable to most of the rest of the world as human. Deadly sin causes the rest of the human community to say: "How can this person do this thing and still be human?"

The events in the former Yugoslavia seem to me to characterize perfectly the results of deadly anger. We outsiders are tormented and bedeviled by unimaginable behavior from people who seemed so very like ourselves. They didn't look like our standard idea of the other: they read the same philosophers as we, and we vacationed among them, enjoying their food, their music, their ordinary pleasantries. And yet, a kind of incomprehensible horror has grown up precisely because of an anger that has gone out of control and has fed on itself until all human eyes are blinded by the bloated flesh of over-gorged anger. People who five years ago ate together, studied together, even married, have sworn to exterminate one another in the most bloody and horrifying ways. Hundreds of years of mutual injustices, treasured like sacred texts, have been gone over, resurrected, nurtured, so that a wholly new creature has been brought to life, a creature bred on anger to the exclusion of vision. Hypnotic, addictive vengeance, action without reflection has taken over like a disease. Thousands upon thousands of women have been raped; impregnation has become a curse, a punishment. The old are starved, beautiful ancient cities destroyed. The original cause of the anger is less important now than the momentum that has built up.

This is the deadly power of anger: it rolls and rolls like a flaming boulder down a hill, gathering mass and speed until any thought of cessation is so far beside the point as to seem hopeless. It is not that there is no cause for the anger; the heavy topsoil of repressed injustice breeds anger better than any other medium. But the causes are lost in the momentum of the anger itself, and in the insatiable compulsion to destroy everything so that the open maw of rage may be fed.

The only way to stop this kind of irrational anger is by an act of equally irrational forgiveness. This is difficult to achieve because anger is exciting and enlivening, and forgiveness is quiet and, like small agriculture or the domestic arts, labor-intensive and yielding of modest fruit. Anger has the glamour of illicit sex, forgiveness the endlessly flexible requirements of a long marriage. Anger feeds a sense of power; forgiveness reminds us of our humbleness—that unpopular commodity, so misunderstood (Uriah Heep is not humble; Felicité in Flaubert's "Simple Heart" is). To forgive is to give up the exhilaration of one's own unassailable rightness. "No cause, no cause," says Cordelia at the end of KING LEAR, enabling the broken father to become a "foolish fond old man." "The great rage . . . is kill'd in him," says the doctor. But Cordelia's words turn a dead place into a garden where they can sit, "God's spies," and wait for what we all wait for, the death that we cannot keep back.

Only the silence and emptiness following a moment of forgiveness can stop the monster of deadly anger, the grotesque creature fed and fattened on innocent blood (and what blood is not, in itself, innocent?). The end of anger requires a darkness, the living darkness at the center of the "nothing" that Lear learns about, the black of Mark

Rothko's last panels, a black that contains in itself, invisible, the germs from which life can reknit itself and spring. Its music is the silence beyond even justice, the peace that passes understanding, rare in a lifetime or an age, always a miracle past our deserving, greater than our words.

Lust

JOHN
UPDIKE

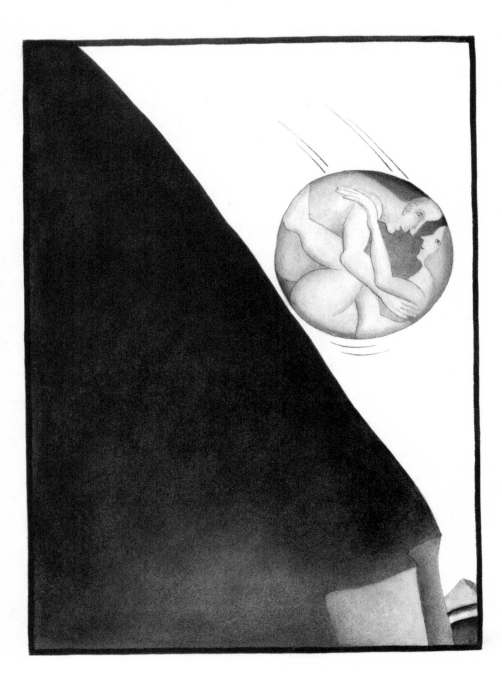

THE

word originally meant pleasure and then was modulated to signify desire and, specifically, sexual desire. How can sexual desire be a sin? Did not God instruct Adam and Eve to be fruitful, and to multiply? Did He not say, having created woman from Adam's rib, that "therefore shall a man leave his father and his mother, and shall cleave unto his wife, and they shall be one flesh"? The singleness of flesh is itself a vivid metaphor for copulation. The organic world is soaked in sex; Lucretius, in his epic ON THE NATURE OF THINGS, begins by saluting Venus: "Yea, through seas and mountains and tearing rivers and the leafy haunts of birds and verdant plains thou dost strike fond love into the hearts of all, and makest them in hot desire to renew the stock of their races, each after his own kind."

Venus alone, in the rousing translation of Cyril Bailey, is "pilot to the nature of things"—without her aid nothing "comes forth into the bright coasts of light, nor waxes glad nor lovely." Two millennia after Lucretius and his fellow Latin celebrants of all-powerful love, Freud and his followers have reconfirmed the helplessly sexual nature of humankind, and have announced the harmfulness, not to say the futility, of sexual repression. How strangely on modern ears falls the notion that lust—sexual desire that wells up in us as involuntarily as saliva—

in itself is wicked! With what nervous hilarity did we greet Jimmy Carter's famous confession: "I've looked on a lot of women with lust. I've committed adultery in my heart many times." Carter was running for President at the time; his opponent, the incumbent Gerald Ford, was a more typical post-Freudian man; asked how often he made love, he healthily responded, "Every chance I get." Impotence, frigidity, un-attractiveness—these are the sins of which we are truly ashamed.

But to the early Christian moralists, of whom St. Paul and Augustine are the greatest, the body was a beast to be tamed, not a master to be served. In that decadent, brutal first-century Roman world, sex possibly did not seem to Paul a very big deal; the world was about to be dissolved in the Second Coming of Christ, and procreation, of such concern to the Old Testament God, was practically irrelevant. The seventh chapter of Paul's first letter to the Corinthians considers briskly the topic the Corinthians proposed: "It is good for a man not to touch a woman." Paul concurs, with a famous qualification: "I say therefore to the unmarried and widows, It is good for them if they abide even as I. But if they cannot contain, let them marry: for it is better to marry than to burn." Augustine had had more experience of burning than Paul: in Carthage's "cauldron of dissolute loves," his CONFESSIONS tell us, he fell "in love with loving." Some chapters after sketching his youthful life and his concubine, he confides to God, "I had prayed to you for chastity and said 'Give me chastity and continence, but not yet.' For I was afraid that you would answer my prayer at once and cure me too soon of the disease of lust, which I wanted satisfied, not quelled."

His youth passed, and the worst of the burning, and he evolved, as an African bishop beset by Donatists and Pelagians, a pessimistic theology that virtually identified human sexuality with original sin. Though Augustine's fiercer insistences (upon infant damnation and predestination, say) reminded other Christians of the Manichaeism to which he had been a convert for a time, his theology became one of the foundations upon which the Church instituted a thousand-year war against the flesh—for saints, mortification, and for the laity, regulation.

It tests the patience of a Protestant to peruse the Catholic Encyclopedia's article on "Lust," with its fussy, imperturbable bureaucratic obstinacy and orderliness. An alleged order, described as natural and rational, is repeatedly invoked: "A lustful action is a disordered use or pursuit of sex pleasure not only because it defeats the biological, social, or moral purpose of sex activity, but also because in doing this it subjects the spiritual in man to values of the grossly material order, acting as a disintegrating force in the human personality." Lust leads to "blindness of mind, rashness, thoughtlessness, inconstancy, self-love, and excessive attachment to the material world." The pitfall of venereal sin resides in "merely sensible" pleasures such as "delight in the touch of a soft object," let alone a human kiss: "the Church has condemned a proposition that states that a kiss indulged for the sake of carnal pleasure and that does not involve danger of further consent is only venially sinful." That is, a kiss is *mortally* sinful. Sexual activity has but two legitimate ends, "the procreation of children and the promotion of the mutual love of spouses in marriage." Narrow and pedantic is the way: we are invited to consider two sinners against the sexual order, "a prostitute who plies her trade for monetary gain without any physical enjoyment, and . . . a married man enjoying normal conjugal intimacy but with no motive except that of physical pleasure." The first sins "against the sex order without a sin of lust," the second commits "a sin of lust without a sin against the sexual order." With pleasure, without pleasure—the whole scene seems damned. What right-thinking man or woman would not quickly abandon so treacherous a minefield for the monastery and the nunnery?

But of course the gospel of Freud has triumphed; the nunneries are drying up, and priests are being hauled into court for their numerous offenses against chastity. Sex is a great disorderer of society—the old ascetics were not wrong about that. The embarrassingly detailed religious prohibitions that strike the modern liberal as outrageous and ridiculous—against masturbation, contraception, homosexuality, and so-called sodomy—were patchwork attempts to wall in the polymorphous-perverse torrents that, in our time, have conspicuously undermined those confining but as yet unreplaced institutions, marriage and the male-headed family. Pornography and its slightly more demure cousin, advertising, present an ideal world, and the claims of the ideal strain and stress imperfect reality. Citizens' private sexual expectations do spill over into society, producing divorce, out-of-wedlock pregnancies, and a rise in literally mortal venereal disease. The conscientious medieval lovers who in the throes of the sex act had to consider whether their concupiscient sensations (*concupiscienta*) were remaining in line with "right reason" (*rectam rationem*) are matched by the modern lovers who must keep asking themselves which bodily fluids might infect what susceptible membranes with the HIV virus. The old nay-sayers were right at least in this: sex has consequences, it is not a holiday from the world.

The sin of lust was defined by St. Thomas as a misalignment with God's procreative purposes; another serene systemizer, Spinoza, wrote in his ETHICS, "Avarice, ambition, lust, etc., are nothing but species of madness." Madness, presumably, is to be avoided, as a deviation from an Aristotelian norm of sane moderation. Of the seven deadly sins, gluttony and sloth are sins of excess, of quantity rather than quality, since the human animal must both eat and rest. It must lust, also, one might say, or else sublimate.

Is lust, however, really as simple, as marginal to our spiritual and mental being, as sleeping and eating? Is it not, as Freud and Augustine darkly agree, central to our Promethean human nature? Lust, which begins in a glance of the eye, is a searching, and its consummation, step by step, a knowing. Not only does the sexual appetite join us to "the beasts of the field" and our chthonian mother—"the Mother of All Living," wrote Robert Graves, "the ancient power of fright and lust"— but it calls into activity our most elegant faculties: of self-display, social intercourse, and internal idealization. We are attracted not merely to the bodies of others but to their psyches, the shimmering non-material identities that used to be called souls. Romantic love, which Denis de Rougemont convincingly described as a pernicious heresy, rarefies lust into an angelic standoff, a fruitless longing without which our energizing circumambient dreamland of song, film, and fiction would be bereft of its main topic. This endless celebration of love and its frustrations is a popular religion, giving dignity and significance to the ephemeral.

Love is supposedly eternal, whereas lust is a physical process that has an end. It rhymes with "dust," a number of poets have noticed. Andrew Marvell begs his "Coy Mistress" to succumb ere "your quaint honour turn to dust; / And into ashes all my lust." But Shakespeare wrote the definitive treatise, in his Sonnet 129, beginning, "Th'expense of spirit in a waste of shame / Is lust in action." Lust is, he goes on, "a swallowed bait" and "A bliss in proof, and proved, a very woe; / Before, a joy proposed—behind, a dream." Yet none, he concludes, "knows well / To shun the heaven that leads men to this hell."

The Bible, actually, is rather soft on lust. Jesus's plea for the adulterous woman and his fondness for female company, high and low, give a genial tinge to His ministry.* The Old Testament contains erotic

---

* A reader of THE NEW YORK TIMES BOOK REVIEW wrote to point out that Jesus also said, in the Sermon on the Mount as recorded by Matthew, "Whosoever looketh on a woman to lust after her hath committed adultery with her already in his heart. And if thy right eye offend thee,

❧

poetry and a number of erotic episodes; King David's lusting after Bathsheba, spied at her bath from a rooftop, led to adultery and the murder of her husband, Uriah the Hittite, but not to any permanent loss of David's status as God's favorite. "The thing that David had done displeased the Lord," and the Lord killed the illicit couple's first-born child, but then Bathsheba gave birth to Solomon. Out of lust, wisdom. If God created the world, He created sex, and one way to construe our inexhaustible sexual interest is as a form of praise of Creation. Says the Song of Solomon: "The joints of thy thighs are like jewels, the work of the hands of a cunning workman."

In admiring another, and in yearning to make our flesh one with the other's, we are stepping out of our skins into a kind of selflessness, and into a sense of beauty. Without lust on the planet, what would wax glad and lovely? Liberal truisms on the joy—nay, the downright virtuousness—of sexual activity are very easy to pen in this day and

---

pluck it out, and cast it from thee: for it is profitable for thee that one of thy members should perish, and not that thy whole body should be cast into hell." As elsewhere in Matthew, Jesus presents an uncharacteristically stern and fierce face. In the Hemingway story "God Rest You Merry, Gentlemen," a sixteen-year-old boy, tormented by "that awful lust," takes the words to heart and cuts off his penis. Most boys, such as Jimmy Carter, stop short of that.

age. What we may lose in this ease is a sense of the majestic power the religious deniers felt, the power of lust to bind souls to this transient, treacherous world, and to drive men and women to heedless extremes of obsession. Sex loses something when we deny its tragic underside. T. S. Eliot wrote of Baudelaire, "He was at least able to understand that the sexual act as evil is more dignified, less boring, than as the natural, 'life-giving', cheery automatism of the modern world. For Baudelaire, sexual operation is at least something not analogous to Kruschen Salts." Humanly enough, some sense of the forbidden—of what Freud spoke of as an "obstacle . . . necessary to swell the tide of libido to its height"—gives lust its savor, its keenness. Such is the confusion of this fallen world, where sins lie intermixed with the seeds of being.

Gluttony

WILLIAM TREVOR

A

few of us meet now and again, not often these days, in the Gran Paradiso or the Café Pelican. Once it was downstairs at Bianchi's, but like so much of London, Bianchi's isn't there anymore.

We're of an age now, no longer young yet not entirely old, eating less than we did, drinking a bit less too, though not by much. We have the past in common, and by chance were once clients of Mr. Pinkerton, an accountant who was passed among us in the 1960's, recommended as a miracle worker. In the Gran Paradiso or the Café Pelican, we invariably end up talking about Mr. Pinkerton—about his small idiosyncrasies, and the ways in which he was different from accountants we have subsequently known. We touch upon the subject of gluttony, since it was gluttony that destroyed him, or so we have always assumed. We wonder about its nature and the form it takes, and if St. Thomas Aquinas was fair to designate it a sin when more charitably it might perhaps have been called an eating disorder. We recall other instances of its excesses and other gluttons we have encountered.

I remember them at school—useful boys who would consume our plates of pudding or the cold, stale teatime sausage rolls on Sundays, the porridge that otherwise ended up behind the radiators. There was a man I once accompanied on a railway journey who, having dined in the restaurant car and vexedly complained about the quality of the food, ordered the same meal all over again. Most memorably, though, there was Mr. Pinkerton.

He was in his fifties when we knew him, a cheerful, sandy-haired man of 308 pounds, with small eyes that were puffed away to pinpricks by inflations of the surrounding flesh. With a wife whom none of us ever met, or even saw, but imagined to be small and wiry, forever in a kitchen overall, he occupied a terraced house in Wimbledon in south-west London. The marriage was a late blossoming for both of them, being only a few months old when I placed my modest financial affairs in Mr. Pinkerton's hands. This was one of the first facts he revealed to me and I received the impression, as others did later, that the house was Mrs. Pinkerton's, that her possession of it had even played a part in her husband's decision to relinquish his bachelor status.

"Peckish, old chap?" Mr. Pinkerton inquired in the small, ornament-clad dining room in which all business was conducted. Without waiting for a response, he was already maneuvering his bulk around the table, on which piles of blank ledger pages, pencils, erasers, a pencil sharpener, and pen and ink had been laid out. A few minutes later he returned with two plates of sandwiches—beef, ham, pickle and cheese, sardine, tomato, cucumber—the white bread cut thickly, the plates piled high. On all my visits to the dining room, the procedure never varied. There could be no settling down to the account sheets until the sandwiches were fetched, and when the evening ended there were plates of buttery currant scones to see the stomach through the night.

Mr. Pinkerton belonged to an age long before that of the computer; indeed, he could be said to have predated the typewriter, since his accounts were prepared and submitted to the Inland Revenue in tiny, neat handwriting. Jotting down expenses—meals taken away from home, a proportion of heating and lighting, travel abroad and in the United Kingdom for professional purposes—he estimated rather than recorded. Receipts or other evidence of expenditure didn't feature in his calculations.

"About six hundred, old chap? Say seven? Eight?" There was an entry called "Spare Copies," which had something to do with the purchase of one's own books for promotional purposes. So at least Mr. Pinkerton's literary clients assumed; we never asked, simply agreed to the figures proposed. But born among the china shepherds and shepherdesses, the Highland cattle and flying geese of that small dining room, the term went into the language and to this day appears on accounts annually submitted to various divisions of the British Inland Revenue. "Wife's salary, old chap?" Mr. Pinkerton would inquire, pen poised again, and would suggest an appropriate sum.

Sometimes he visited me rather than I him. He would arrive in the house in the evening, invited to supper because there was hospitality to be returned. He always came on foot, crossing the two commons that separated our neighborhood from his, accompanied by a retriever that matched, proportionally, his own great size, and carrying a stout black stick ("for protection, old chap"). On the first of these occasions, when we sat down to eat, he asked for "a couple of slices of bread" to go with the potatoes, vegetables, and meat, and throughout the meal the request was several times repeated. On future occasions my wife anticipated the demand by placing within his reach a sliced loaf that he always managed to finish, chomping his way through it while also consuming whatever else was on offer. "Shouldn't refer to another client, of course," he would say between mouthfuls, and then give us details of a case he was conducting in some northern town, its outcome relevant since he hoped for the establishing of a precedent. "Tax inspector up a gum tree," he would confidently predict, a favorite expression that was always accompanied by a gurgle of mirth. "Friendly cunning" was a favorite also, the weapon of his attack in taxation matters.

By way of further variation as to rendezvous, Mr. Pinkerton occasionally suggested a meeting in a public house, the big, old-fashioned Henekey's in Holborn where, ensconced in a booth, he ate an inordinate number of Scotch eggs and a couple of plates of potato salad. He once told me that these were the only foods he touched in a public house, they being the only barroom dishes that were "safe." I wasn't entirely sure what he meant by that, nor were the clients among whom his gourmandizing eventually became a talking point. We passed on his predilections when, without embarrassment, they were revealed to one or other of us—a particular fondness for a well-roasted parsnip, how he never left the house in Wimbledon without a supply of iced biscuits in his pockets, how he liked to indulge in a midmorning feast of tea and fruitcake, how he had once in someone's presence eaten forty-one sausages.

Gluttony has been numbered among the deadly sins we live with, presumably because it exemplifies an absence of the restraint that dignifies the human condition. Like its six companions, it is at best unattractive. The boys who waded into accumulations of pudding were popular in the dining hall but despised outside it. The two-dinners man in the restaurant car caused revulsion in the features of the waiters. Eyes looked the other way when Mr. Pinkerton reached out for his forty-first sausage.

~Even so, in his case we were not censorious. He conducted our affairs with efficiency and was a card as well. We were fond of him because he was mysterious and eccentric, because he enlivened the routine of the work he did for us with the fruits of a prodigious memory, storing away matchbox information and sometimes appearing to know us better than we knew ourselves. "August twenty-sixth, 1952. Day you were married, old chap. A Tuesday, if memory serves." He was always right. If you had to cancel a meeting because of a dentist's appointment, the date and time were recorded forever. "Morning of July fourth, old chap. Upper molar, left, dispatched." All of it, for us, was leaven in the weight of figures and assessments and final demands, and none of us guessed that something was the matter. He was a big man; he ate in order to fill that bulky frame. It never occurred to us that his appetite lay fatally at the heart of his existence, like a cruel tumor.

It is only in retrospect that the bloated figure seems lonely, that the passion that ordered its peculiarities seems in some way sinister. It is only in retrospect that we can speculate with clarity on Mr. Pinkerton's downfall, which for me began as an unheeded intimation on a Sunday morning in 1967 when he tried to borrow 500 pounds. The request came out of the blue, on the telephone, and such was my faith in Mr. Pinkerton's respectability and his professional acumen that I said, of course. I did not yet know that a number of his clients had just been touched for similar sums. Some obliged; others more wisely did not.

As the months went by, the loans remained unpaid and, even worse, the Inland Revenue's Final Notices were now being followed by threats of Immediate Court Action or Distraint on Goods. Men with bowler hats even arrived at some of our houses. "Not to worry, old chap" was Mr. Pinkerton's endlessly repeated response, followed by soothing promises that he would, that very day, speak to the relevant inspector, who had by the sound of things got himself up a gum tree.

But this time he didn't tramp round to the local tax office with his dog and his stick and his old black briefcase. Instead, all over London, Mr. Pinkerton's clients were in trouble, summoned to the revenue courts, reprimanded, investigated, penalized. Mr. Pinkerton's telephone was cut off; he no longer answered letters. At the behest of a new

❧

accountant, I went to see him in Wimbledon one cold winter's morning, hoping to collect some of my papers.

Mr. Pinkerton was in rags. He had been doing the fires, he explained, leading me into the dining room, but there was no sign of anything like that. "Had a burglary, old chap," he said when I asked about my papers, and when I suggested that surely no burglar would steal material as worthless as account sheets, he simply added that he and Mrs. Pinkerton had experienced the misfortune to have had a fire as well. I wanted to ask him what the matter was, why he was talking about events that clearly hadn't occurred, but somewhere in his small eyes there was a warning that this was private territory, so I desisted.

I never saw him again, but from time to time a fragmentary record of his subsequent career was passed about, downstairs in Bianchi's in those days. The house in Wimbledon was seized by a mortgage company; he was struck off as an accountant; he and Mrs. Pinkerton were in paupers' lodgings. There was a theory that he had destroyed all the papers in his care—a form of symbolic suicide—and a year or so later death was there for real—he died in the streets one day.

Our speculations mourn him. "Peckish, old chap?" comes the echo from his heyday, the question asked of himself after dinner with a client. Tins of peas and beans and meatballs, beetroot in vinegar, cold apple dumpling are laid out to see the stomach through the night. And later on, in dreams, his table's spread again, with meats and soups and celery in parsley sauce, with cauliflower and leeks and roasted parsnips, potatoes mashed and fried, crème brulée, crème caramel, meringues and brandy snaps, mints and Turkish delight.

If some, we wonder, are selected to be the recipients of the gifts that lift humanity to its heights, can it be said that others are chosen to bear the burdens by which some balance may be struck? And we wonder if the gluttony we knew was a form of disguise or compensation for an inner emptiness, if the burden that is called a sin was more complicated than it seemed to be. We mull uncertainly over that, although we knew the man quite well, and in the end we leave the question unresolved, as somehow it seems meant to be. Blue-suited and courteous, the stout accountant went gratefully to the grave. In the Gran Paradiso or the Café Pelican, with his ghost among us, he hints at that.

Pride

GORE
VIDAL

IS

pride a sin at all? The Oxford English Dictionary strikes a primly English note: "A high or overweening opinion of one's own qualities, attainments or estate," or too clever by half, the ultimate put-down in those bright arid islands where ignorance must be lightly worn.

Apparently, the Romans and the Greeks had other, by no means pejorative, words for it. The quintessential Greek, Odysseus, reveled in being too clever by any number of halves. Of course, neither Greeks nor Romans had a word for sin, a Judeo-Christian concept that the Germans did have a word for, *Sunde*, which Old English took aboard. Obviously, in any time and place an overweening person is tiresome, but surely laughter is the best tonic for restoring him to our common weeniness. He hardly needs to be prayed for or punished as a sinner. Yet pride is listed as the first of the seven deadly sins, and only recently—by accident, not design—did I figure out why.

Over the years I have taken some . . . well, pride in never reading from my own work, or appearing with other writers on public occasions, or joining any organizations other than labor unions. In 1976, when I was elected to the National Institute of Arts and Letters, I promptly declined this high estate on the ground that I was already a member of the Diners' Club. John Cheever was furious with me:

"Couldn't you have at least said Carte Blanche? Diners' Club is so tacky." A couple of months ago I declined election to the Society of American Historians—politely, I hope.

James Joyce's "silence, exile, and cunning" is the ultimate in artist's pride. But for someone politically inclined, that was not possible; even so, one could still play a lone hand, as a writer if not as an engaged citizen. Recently, Norman Mailer asked me if I would join him and two other writers in a reading of George Bernard Shaw's DON JUAN IN HELL. The proceeds would go to the Actors Studio. I would play the Devil, who has most of the good lines.

So, out of Charity—Vanity?—I set to one side my proud rule and shared a stage with three writers and the fading ghost of a very great one; fading because Shaw can appeal only to those who think that human society can be made better by human intelligence and will. I am of Shaw's party; the Devil's, too, I found, as I began to immerse myself in the part.

In a very long speech, the Devil makes an attractive case for himself; he also explains the bad press that he has got from the celestial hordes and their earthly admirers. The Devil believes that the false view of him in England is the result of an Italian and an Englishman. The

Italian, of course, is Dante, and the Englishman is John Milton. Somewhat gratuitously, Shaw's Devil remarks that like everyone else he has never managed to get all the way through PARADISE LOST and PARADISE REGAINED. Although I had my problems with the second, the first is the masterpiece of our language, and Lucifer, the Son of Morning, blazes most attractively while God seems more arbitrary and self-regarding than ever, eager in His solipsistic pride to hear only praise from the angelic choirs, as well as from Adam and Eve, two mud pies He liked to play with.

It is Milton's conceit that proud Lucifer, a bored angel, tempts Adam and Eve with the only thing a totalitarian ruler must always keep from his slaves, knowledge. Rather surprisingly, the First Couple choose knowledge—well, she chooses it; lose Eden; go forth to breed and die while Lucifer and his party, expelled from heaven, fall and fall and fall through Chaos and Old Night until they reach rock bottom, hell:

> Here we may reign secure, and in my choice
> To reign is worth ambition though in hell:
> Better to reign in hell than serve in heav'n.

I first heard those words in 1941, spoken by Edward G. Robinson in the film of Jack London's SEA-WOLF. It was like an electrical shock. The great alternative. I can do no other. Bright world elsewhere. To reign and not to serve. To say, No. This was my introduction to Milton and to Lucifer's pride.

I was brought up in a freethinking Southern family where pride of clan could lead to all sorts of folly as well as to exemplary self-sacrifice.

My great-grandfather sat for a whole day on the steps of the courthouse at Walthall, Miss., debating whether to go fight with the rest of the clan in a civil war that he knew could not be won, and for a cause that he despised. Pride required him to fight with his clan; he fell at Shiloh.

Fifty years later, in the Senate, his son defied the leader of his party, President Woodrow Wilson, on the issue of whether or not the United States should fight in World War I. The Chamber of Commerce of Oklahoma City sent him a telegram saying that if he did not support the war, he would be an ex-senator. He sent them a telegram: "How many of your membership are of draft age?" He fell from office, as they had promised.

There is a whiff of sulfur here, perhaps; but there is also the sense that one is the final judge of what must be done despite the seductive temptations and stern edicts of the gods. In the absence of a totalitarian sky-god or earthly ruler, there is the always troubling dictatorship of the American majority, which Tocqueville saw as the dark side to our "democracy."

Very much in the family tradition, in 1948, I ran counter to the majority's loony superstitions about sex and fell quite far indeed. (This newspaper's regular daily critic not only did not review the offending novel, THE CITY AND THE PILLAR, but told my publisher that he would never again read, much less review, a book of mine: six subsequent books were not reviewed in the daily paper.) But pride required that I bear witness, like it or not, and if the superstitious masses—or great Zeus himself—disapproved, I would go even deeper into rebellion, and fall farther. Understandably, for the cowed majority, pride is the most unnerving "sin" because pride scorns them quite as much as Lucifer did God.

Significantly, a story that keeps cropping up from culture to culture is that of the man who steals fire from heaven to benefit the human race. After Prometheus stole the fire for us, he ended up chained to a rock, an eagle gnawing eternally at his liver. Zeus' revenge was terrible, but the Prometheus of Aeschylus does not bend; in fact, he curses Zeus and predicts: "Let him act, let him reign his little while as he will; for he shall not long rule over the gods."

So let us celebrate pride when it defies those dominations and powers that enslave us. In my own case, for a quarter-century I have refused to read, much less write for, this newspaper, but, as Prometheus also somewhat cryptically observes, "Time, growing ever older, teaches all things." Or, as Dr. Johnson notes, reflecting Matthew's Gospel, "Pride must have a fall"; thus proving it was the real thing and not merely the mock.

 Avarice

1849: A Distraction

RICHARD
HOWARD

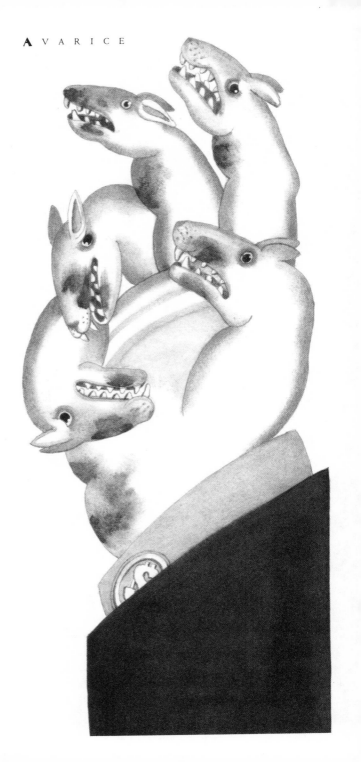

MY

dear Balzac, you must remain quite still.

    Make no motion at all, or nothing

will appear on the plate but a faint grisaille,

    the Unknown Masterpiece indeed!

Though mine is a drastically lesser gift,

    let me attempt to entertain you

or at least to keep your spirit occupied

    while the flesh is forcibly idle.

Between exposures (that is our rakish name

    for the interval when light's pencil

is permitted to limn your face) you may speak,

    but you must not shift your attitude;

I have found that unobtrusive clamp behind

    the nape to be of great assistance—

don't you agree? Then let us begin. Of course

    I have hoped for such an occasion

in order to speculate with you . . . Oh no,

    nothing like an interrogation,

merely these musings intended to beguile

an intellect that has awed all France.

Ready now? No moving until I signal . . .

It has been, sir, a constant bewilderment

    since I first came to the "Comedy"

—reading for over a decade now—that you,

    having anatomized Greed as well

as Molière, abstain from all condemnation;

    and that an author who engenders

such unflagging monsters of Avarice as

    a Grandet, a Gobseck, a Goriot!

nonetheless hits off his dismaying portraits

    of all that is worst in humankind

without a single condemnation of sin—

    as if the creator draws no line

between Avarice and Wanting? Book after

    book declares all human happiness

comes down to numbers, figures, sums—as if

    counting were the same thing as loving!

No, no, don't speak yet! Not till the plate records

a face that contradicts all logic:

the parts so much greater than the whole . . . Indulge

my lens but one more moment, then

you may correct my views as wisdom sees fit:

if Not To Have is the onset of Desire,

then isn't actual having—such *owning*

as you so exhaustively articulate—

isn't possessing in that kind . . . culpable?

Now you may speak, but please to retain

the same pose, we must attempt at least one more . . .

Nadar, dear fellow, you do not read me well.

In literature, who can believe

he has ever been understood? We all die

alone. See here: when you speak the word

AVARICE, *when you utter the verb* TO HAVE,

feel how fondly your front teeth caress

your lower lip; that is how the meaning comes,

our bodies making out, making up

the sense of words. . . . Our senses make it: AVID!

my friend, as eager to own the self

as the mouth to own the tongue. Read me better:

I see no sin in loving what we own,

for indeed we own nothing save what owns us——

our tongues, for instance——we own nothing!

The one sin is to believe, indeed behave

as if we own what we love: I wrote

as much a million times, I shall keep writing,

but people do not willingly read

if they can find something else to amuse them——

every parent can conceive the fun

of abusing a child . . . no book is needed.

You cannot call such misers as mine

sinners——they are merely exaggerations

of our mutual weakness, for they

still cannot believe they own what they covet.

Sin is supposing we can possess

our passions . . . Suppose we try another now:

I understand, hearing you speak so,

that all human knowledge is guilty knowledge,

and the only consequence is flight!

Eyes here, so! Then afterwards... *Afterwards*

you will sell me the plate. I must own it:

I must have myself. Nadar, the going rate?

Publisher's Note: Everyone who was anyone in French culture
in the nineteenth century posed for Nadar's camera. Everyone
except for Honoré de Balzac. But among Nadar's proudest
possessions was this daguerreotype of Balzac made by an un-
identified photographer around 1845, five years before the
author's death.

Envy

A.S.
BYATT

"THROUGH

envy of the Devil," says the Wisdom of Solomon, came death into the world. And envy was the cause of the first murder and the first death, in the biblical narrative, when "the Lord had respect unto Abel and to his offering, but unto Cain and to his offering he had not respect." Envy is the sin that festers in hierarchies and families, in structured societies of all kinds.

The tragedy, personal and national, of KING LEAR is driven by sibling rivalry. "He always loved our sister most," says Goneril, "and with what poor judgment He hath now cast her off appears too grossly." And Edmund, the attractive villain of the play, cannot decide between resentment of his place in the family and resentment of his position in society as the reason for his wickedness. He is both a bastard and "some twelve or fourteen moonshines lag of a brother," and finds both of these intolerable.

Envy grows in the deprived and in those who consider themselves deprived. In our time the phrase "the politics of envy" has been much bandied about by the right wing and by threatened élites. All sins have their contrary virtues for which they are sometimes mistaken: love and lust, prudence and avarice, self-respect and pride, righteous indignation

❦

and anger, caution and sloth, good fellowship and greed. The contrary virtue of envy is justice.

Small children, angry with siblings or playmates, cry out, "It isn't *fair!*" The idea of fairness comes earlier to them than the recognition of envy, and it is a good and right idea. The poor, the helpless, the uneducated, the unloved also cry out, "It isn't *fair!*" and if fairness means anything they are right. Yet the politics of envy also exists in families and in states. There is a moral knife-edge in a class where no child may take home spelling homework because some children come from homes where they will receive no help from their parents.

Psychoanalysts are strong on envy. Freud invented penis envy to explain female discontent, and found it the most intractable symptom he had to deal with. In "Analysis Terminable and Interminable," he writes of women he cannot cure, because they feel "an inner conviction that the analysis will avail them nothing and that they will be none the better for it." And, he adds, "we can only agree with them when we discover that their strongest motive in coming for treatment was the hope that they might somehow still obtain a male organ, the lack of which is so painful to them." In English the word "envy" is related to the French *envie*, which means desire. But in German the uncompromising *Penisneid* means envy, the grudge, the sin.

Melanie Klein, in a late work, ENVY AND GRATITUDE, diagnoses the infant's envy of the "creativity" of the good, life-giving, nourishing breast. The infant, who is dependent on it, resents that dependence and fantasizes about ingesting or destroying the organ. Both Freud and Klein are sublimely in possession of the envied part, penis or breast, and godlike in their dismissal of their envious or denying patients. Klein equates the analyst's good interpretations with the nourishing milk that is rejected or ignored by the recalcitrant patient. She is almost the mother goddess whose children, like Cain or Satan, question her judgments. And Freud's own term, *Penisneid*, one might argue in this context, has taken on a snaky allegorical personality of its own.

Allegory is an archaic artistic method, and the deadly sins are at their liveliest in the personified parades of the Middle Ages and the Renaissance. People in those remote days believed in number mysticism, and in essences and faculties. The forms who writhe and glare and threaten in blood and slime and smoke from church walls and sermons are neither as lively now as ghosts and demons nor as interesting as the forces in which we really believe, the Oedipus complex and racism. I once began a thesis on allegory because I was interested in narratives that divided human lives into warring fleshed abstractions—so very different from the psychological novels of Proust or the psychobiological tropisms desiderated by Nathalie Sarraute.

In Spenser's FAERIE QUEENE, there are varying levels of reality, from stories on tapestries that move to dreamed crocodiles in temples. The Redcrosse Knight in the House of Pride encounters all the deadly sins, led by Lucifera, the Whore of Babylon, alias Pride, alias the Roman Catholic Church, and probably alias Mary, Queen of Scots, riding the apocalyptic Dragon. In this parade, Envy rides on a wolf, chewing a venomous toad, and also secretly chewing "his owne mawe." He is dressed in a discolored garment covered with eyes, and a "hatefull Snake" is curled secretly in his bosom. He "grudged at" the felicity of his own company, and particularly hates good writers: "He does backebite and spightfull poison spues From leprous mouth on all that ever writt."

He is less real than the Knight, or the true and false ladies whom he levels with, and is there to be sensuously enjoyed for his metaphorical vigor. Wolves, snakes, toads, and self-consumption go with envy, as pigs and vine leaves and sweat go with gluttony. It is curious how the iconography remains constant through the shape-shifts of the figure.

One of the early and powerful depictions of envy occurs in Ovid's METAMORPHOSES. Ovid's story is also one of sibling rivalry. It is about the human sisters Herse and Aglauros, the gods Minerva and Mercury, and Envy. Beautiful Herse is loved by Mercury. Envious Aglauros has profaned the secrets of Minerva and won't allow Mercury to enter her father's palace. Minerva summons Envy to deal with her. A simple creature, neither god nor human, Envy is a personified abstraction. She lives in a cavern wrapped in thick black fog, and eats snakes' flesh: "Her eyes are all awry, her teeth are foul with mould; green poisonous gall overflows her breast, and venom drips from her tongue. She never smiles, save at the sight of another's troubles; she never sleeps, disturbed with wakeful cares; unwelcome to her is the sight of men's success, and with the sight she pines away: she gnaws and is gnawed, herself her own punishment."

As with all allegorical persons, the intense solidity of the bodily presence is the meaning. At Minerva's bidding, Envy flies toward Aglauros, blighting fields, tall trees, and whole cities with her foul breath. What she does to Aglauros is to turn her into an image of Envy herself.

She breathes her foul breath into the girl, who is consumed by envy of her sister, as if by secret flames in a damped-down bonfire of weeds, until Hermes finally solidifies her into a frozen attitude at the palace door: "There she sat, a lifeless statue. Nor was the stone white in color: her soul had stained it black."

Aglauros is a sister of all the ugly sisters of fairy tales, who envy their industrious beautiful sisters who visit fairies and come back speaking gold coins. The ugly sisters are lazy and inert, they do not help old women or trapped animals, they speak venomous toads and snakes, and they are turned to stone. Allegory and fairy tales are solidified morals and psychology, and in the case of envy they work particularly well, because envy works by paralysis and self-consumption—the envious do indeed become Envy.

I am sorry, personally, about the pervasively bad images of snakes and toads, creatures both energetic and peaceful, but there are centuries of human symbolism against me. One of my favorite mythological snakes is the serpent Nidhogg, who lives in the dark caverns under the Scandinavian World-Ash, and perpetually gnaws its roots. I had hopes that he, too, was a personification of primeval envy, and that Nid was cognate with the German *Neid*, so that Nidhogg might be a relation of

Penisneid, a primeval denial and rejection. *Nid* is indeed Danish for envy, though my Danish translator tells me that on balance scholars seem to think that Nidhogg represents the waning moon, "the period when dark is at its darkest." *Nid* is the Norse word for waning, and *hoggr* is one who strikes down, or fells.

When I first began to think about envy, the examples that came to mind were from the nineteenth century, and the energy of Ovid's foul-breathed destroyer does seem to crop up again in some of the proliferating, struggling, simplified creatures who people the worlds of Balzac's HUMAN COMEDY and the novels of Dickens. Perhaps the most condensed and perfect example of the energy of denial and self-consumption is Robert Browning's poem "Soliloquy of the Spanish Cloister." It is very funny and grotesquely black—the soliloquizing monk directs all his ingenuity, all his thought, all his life, to the destruction of the innocent and saintly Brother Lawrence, weaving fantastic plots to trap him into damning heresy on his deathbed, meanwhile secretly ripping off the buds of his melon plants:

Gr-r-r—there go, my heart's abhorrence! Water your damned
flower-pots, do!

If hate killed men, Brother Lawrence, God's blood, would not
mine kill you!

It is characteristic of the hatred inspired by envy that its object is
both innocent and ignorant of that hatred's existence. Brother Lawrence
has done nothing—he just is, busy and fulfilled. Envy destroys the
envious, but it can become part of an elaborate and in a way pointless
plot of destruction.

Balzac's Cousin Bette is a perfect example of this kind of moral
structure—a character so bristling with the secret force of hatred and
malignity that Bette Davis (whose real name was Ruth Elizabeth) is
said to have chosen her stage name in the character's honor. COUSIN
BETTE is part of the "Poor Relations" section of Balzac's great novel-
series. As Shakespeare loaded the dice against Edmund by making him
both a bastard and a younger brother, so Balzac makes Bette doubly
(or trebly) deprived, by making her plain, poor, and eaten up by envy
of her good and beautiful cousin Adeline, who has made a "fortunate"
marriage to Baron Hulot. As Jesus showed psychological accuracy in
making the servant with the single talent the one who buried it and
made nothing of it, so Balzac shows Bette's hatred as the limited energy

of the have-nots. Envy, as I said, is the sin of families and hierarchical societies.

When Balzac first lets us into the mind of Bette, he tells us she had given up hope of competing with her cousin: "But envy remained hidden in her heart, like a plague germ which may come to life and devastate a city if the fatal bale of wool in which it lies hidden is ever opened." And a few pages later he says: "She was still the child who had tried to tear her cousin's nose off, and who, if she had not learned rational behavior, would perhaps have killed her in a paroxysm of jealousy."

Bette, Balzac says, is like a savage. "The savage has only emotions," he writes. "The civilized man has emotions plus ideas. In the savage, the brain receives, one may conclude, few impressions, so that he is at the mercy of one all-pervading emotion. . . . Cousin Bette, a primitive peasant from Lorraine and not without a strain of treachery, had a nature of this savage kind, a kind that is commoner among the masses than is generally supposed and that may explain their behavior during revolutions."

Here political and personal envy—or an obsessive desire for fairness—merge again. Bette, in fact, helps to engineer the destruction of her cousin's family life and fortune, and the destruction of her cousin's daughter's marriage, by encouraging Baron Hulot's philandering and the machinations of the courtesan Valérie Marneffe, while she herself remains a gruff, "honest" decentric member of the family circle. Even though Baron Hulot is one of the great literary depictions of compulsive lust, Balzac names his novel after the spinster, the old maid, the single-mindedly envious Cousin Bette. And it is remarkable that none of Bette's victims ever come to know her treachery or to suspect the emotions that eat her up. Envy works inwardly; concealment is part of its nature.

Dickens's masterpiece in the depiction of envy is probably Uriah Heep, though Orlick in GREAT EXPECTATIONS, whose whole existence is inarticulate resentment culminating in murderous violence, is a particularly concentrated example of the same vice. Like Heep, Orlick is in the family but inferior, a sort of servant, someone on the edge, jealous of imagined privileges, full of imagined slights. But where Orlick is solid and thick and menacing, Heep is baroque, lurid, almost an allegorical vice or sin capering in a pageant or on a fresco. He insinuates himself like a snake into the family of his employer, Mr. Wickfield, whom he ostensibly helps but in fact assiduously destroys. Like Bette, like Iago, like Edmund, he represents himself as one of the poor in spirit. Heep and his frightful mother know their "place" in the hierarchy, they repeat and repeat with menacing monotony that they are "umble."

Heep carries the snake imagery in his own body. He writhes, he serpentines. Copperfield watches him with helpless suspicion: "He said nothing at all. He stirred his coffee round and round; he sipped it; he felt his chin softly with his grisly hand; he looked at the fire; he looked about the room; he gasped rather than smiled at me; he writhed and undulated about, in his deferential servility; he stirred and sipped again, but he left the renewal of the conversation to me."

The night on which Heep manages to stay over in Copperfield's chambers is wonderfully comic, and also sinister. "Having lent him a nightcap, which he put on at once, and in which he made such an awful figure that I have never worn one since," Copperfield says, "I left him to his rest."

Copperfield cannot sleep. He dozes. "When I awoke, the recollection that Uriah was lying in the next room sat heavy on me like a waking nightmare, and oppressed me with a leaden dread, as if I had some meaner quality of devil for a lodger.

"The poker got into my dozing thoughts besides, and wouldn't come out. I thought, between sleeping and waking, that it was still red hot, and I had snatched it out of the fire, and run him through the body. I was so haunted at last by the idea, though I knew there was nothing in it, that I stole into the next room to look at him. There I saw him, lying on his back, with his legs extending to I don't know where, gurglings taking place in his throat, stoppages in his nose, and his mouth open like a post-office. He was so much worse in reality than in my distempered fancy that afterwards I was attracted to him in very repulsion, and could not help wandering in and out every half hour or so, and taking another look at him. Still, the long, long night seemed heavy and hopeless as ever, and no promise of day was in the murky sky."

This is brilliant. Heep, the "meaner quality of devil," creates a hell around him, complete with red-hot poker, leaden dread, and a heavy sky. He is a Victorian version of a medieval demon. I had always, since childhood, thought of him as Envy, but recently I began to wonder if he was not Avarice, Hypocrisy, or Lust instead. Heep steals fortunes; he desires Agnes Wickfield for a wife. And then at the end, when he is unmasked by those virtuous innocents Traddles and Micawber, the reason for Heep's actions is revealed. Traddles says: " 'A most remarkable circumstance is that I really don't think he grasped this sum even so much for the gratification of his avarice, which was inordinate, as in the hatred he felt for Copperfield. He said so to me, plainly. He said he would even have spent as much, to baulk or injure Copperfield.' "

Both Copperfield and Heep are additions to the Wickfield household, but whereas Copperfield the gentleman is accepted as a surrogate son and brother, Heep is the servant and the inferior. He is umble and vengeful, a rejected child and a subordinate. He hates Copperfield as Bette hates her cousin. He is an incarnation of envy.

Bette and Uriah are caricatures, monomaniacs verging on personification. The greatest example of envy in literature is Iago, honest Iago, the manipulator and destroyer of an intense love he cannot have or understand, the subordinate who is passed over for Cassio. He is greater than Bette or Heep, because there is no element of caricature about him, no element of personification. He is horribly ordinary, horribly real, horribly limited, horribly busy. He says in Act I of *Othello*, explaining his plotting:

I hate the Moor,

And it is thought abroad, that 'twixt my sheets

He has done my office; I know not if't be true.

But I, for mere suspicion in that kind,

Will do as if for surety: he holds me well,

The better shall my purpose work on him.

Cassio's a proper man, let me see now,

To get his place, and to plume up my will,

In double knavery.

Coleridge's analysis of this passage is brilliant. He says: "The motive-hunting of motiveless malignity—how awful! In itself fiendish; while yet he was allowed to bear the divine image, too fiendish for his own steady view. A being next to devil, only not quite devil—and this Shakespeare has attempted—executed—without disgust, without scandal!"

More recent scholars have wanted to question this. They have claimed that honest Iago was indeed honestly jealous, that Othello had seduced Iago's wife, that there is no mystery about his evil. But Coleridge was surely right. Melanie Klein discusses the difference between envy and jealousy, quoting Crabb's ENGLISH SYNONYMES, in which

Crabb says, "Jealousy fears to lose what it has; envy is pained at seeing another have that which it wants for itself." Jealousy, Klein says, is popularly less hated than envy because jealousy can include a genuine love for "the good." She is herself inclined to see jealousy and envy as closely related, and quotes, without attributing the quotation to a speaker: "But jealous souls will not be answer'd so; They are not ever jealous for the cause, But jealous for they are jealous; 'tis a monster Begot upon itself, born on itself."

The speaker here, however, is not Iago but his wife, Emilia, addressing Desdemona, who replies "Heaven keep that monster from Othello's mind!" It is Iago who has put the monster there, and in Othello's mind "the cause" does visit. Before he kills his wife, he cries out, "It is the cause, it is the cause, my soul!" Othello is jealous, enraged because he loves, not wisely but too well, because he is trusting, and is betrayed and deceived. Iago is merely envious, and envy is bleaker and more insidious and more destructive than jealousy. Writing this essay, I came to see OTHELLO, among other things, as a study in the contrast between the force of jealousy and the meanness of envy. When Iago comes to put Cassio's death in motion, he remarks: "It must not be; if Cassio do remain/He has a daily beauty in his life/That makes me ugly."

This is pure envy, perfectly described. When Iago is unmasked, too late he attracts both the serpentine and the demonic imagery that go with Envy:

> LODOVICO: Where is that viper? Bring the villain forth. . . .
> OTHELLO: Will you, I pray, demand that demi-devil
> Why he hath thus ensnared my soul and body?
> IAGO: Demand me nothing, what you know you know,
> From this time forth I never will speak word.

It is characteristic of the kind of evil Iago embodies that it returns to stubborn inertia, to stony passivity, to silence, as opposed to the violence of Othello's passion and fear of damnation. Lodovico's final characterization of the now-silent Iago is one of Shakespeare's most surprising and wonderful lines. It moves Iago's wickedness out of the personal realm into the world of abstract, natural, terrible forces, where it takes on its real terror. Envy is petty. Iago is "more fell than anguish, hunger or the sea."

In the Judeo-Christian tradition, Satan's envy of God's new favored children, Adam and Eve, brought sibling rivalry and death into the world. Milton's Satan is evil and toadlike when he is envious—he is often romantic and heroic when he is exhibiting pride. Nietzsche, with his mixture of sharp intelligence and wild extravagance, sees the idea of evil, the Evil One, as a creation of the *ressentiment* of the slaves and the poor. His description of "the man of *ressentiment*" might do for all my minor and demi-devils, Heep and Iago, Herse and Bette:

"While the noble man lives in trust and openness with himself . . . the man of *ressentiment* is neither upright nor naive nor honest and straightforward with himself. His soul squints: his spirit loves hiding places, secret paths and back doors, everything covert strikes him as his world, his security, his refreshment; he understands how to keep silent, how not to forget, how to wait, how to be provisionally self-deprecating and humble."

The man of *ressentiment*, Nietzsche concludes, conceives of evil as what oppresses him, creates a contrary vision of "the evil enemy," the Evil One. Nietzsche argues that this enemy is necessarily the opposite of the humble man; he is the "noble man" cast as source of harm and damage. Without following him all the way, we may see how his psy-

❀

chology fits both the psychoanalytic descriptions of the rejecting pro-
jections of envy, and the dangerous hatred of siblings and underlings.
The envious become Envy. By envy of Satan came death into the world.
By envy of children and the weak came Satan into the world, more fell
than anguish, hunger or the sea.

Despair

JOYCE

CAROL

OATES

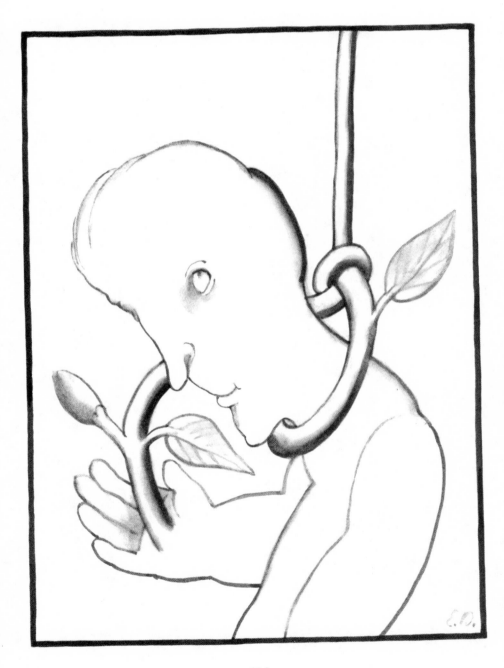

WHAT

mysterious cruelty in the human soul, to have invented despair as a "sin"! Like the Seven Deadly Sins employed by the medieval Roman Catholic Church to terrify the faithful into obedience, despair is most helpfully imagined as a mythical state. It has no quantifiable existence; it "is" merely allegory, yet no less lethal for the fact. Unlike other sins, however, despair is by tradition the sole sin that cannot be forgiven: it is the conviction that one may be damned absolutely, thus a refutation of the Christian savior and a challenge to God's infinite capacity for forgiveness. The sins for which one may be forgiven—pride, anger, lust, sloth, avarice, gluttony, envy—are all firmly attached to objects of this world, but despair seems to bleed out beyond the confines of the immediate ego-centered self and to relate to no desire, no-thing. The alleged sinner has detached himself even from the possibility of sin as a human predilection, and this the Church as the self-appointed voice of God on earth cannot allow.

Religion is organized power in the seemingly benevolent guise of the "sacred" and power is, as we know, chiefly concerned with its own preservation. Its structures, its elaborate rituals and customs and scriptures and commandments and ethics, its very nature, objectify human experience, insisting that what is *out there* in the world is of unquestionably greater significance than what is *in here* in the human spirit. Despair, surely the least aggressive of sins, is dangerous to the totalitarian temperament because it is a state of intense inwardness, thus independence. The despairing soul is a rebel.

So, too, suicide, the hypothetical consequence of extreme despair, has long been a mortal sin in Church theology, in which it is equivalent to murder. Suicide has an element of the forbidden, the obscene, the taboo about it, as the most willful and the most defiantly antisocial of human acts. While thinkers of antiquity condoned suicide, in certain circumstances at least—"In all that you do or say or think, recollect that at any time the power of withdrawal from life is in your hands," Marcus Aurelius wrote in the MEDITATIONS—the Church vigorously punished suicides in ways calculated to warn others and to confirm, posthumously, their despair: bodies were sometimes mutilated, burial in consecrated soil was of course denied, and the Church, ever resourceful, could confiscate goods and land belonging to suicides.

Yet how frustrating it must have been, and be, the attempt to outlaw and punish *despair*—of all sins!

(In fact, one wonders: is "despair" a pathology we diagnose in people who seem to have repudiated our own life-agendas, as "narcissism" is the charge we make against those who fail to be as intrigued by us as we had wished?)

At the present time, despair as a "sin" is hardly convincing. As a state of intense inwardness, however, despair strikes us as a spiritual and moral experience that cuts across superficial boundaries of language, culture, and history. No doubt, true despair is mute and unreflective as flesh lacking consciousness; but the *poetics* of despair have been transcendentally eloquent:

The difference between Despair
And Fear—is like the One—
Between the instant of a Wreck—
And when the Wreck has been—

The Mind is smooth—no Motion—
Contented as the Eye
Upon the Forehead of a Bust—
That knows—it cannot see—

—*Emily Dickinson*

❦

This condition, which might be called a stasis of the spirit, in which life's energies are paralyzed even as life's physical processes continue, is the essence of literary despair. The plunging world goes its own way, the isolated consciousness of the writer splits from it, as if splitting from the body itself. Despair as this state of keenly heightened inwardness has always fascinated the writer, whose subject is after all the imaginative reconstruction of language. The ostensible subject *out there* is but the vehicle, or the pretext, for the ravishing discoveries to be made *in here* in the activity of creating.

Literary despair is best contemplated during insomniac nights. And perhaps most keenly savored during adolescence, when insomnia can have the aura of the romantic and the forbidden; when sleepless nights can signal rebellion against a placidly sleeping—un-conscious—world. At such times, inner and outer worlds seem to merge; insights that by day would be lost define themselves like those phosphorescent minerals coarse and ordinary in the light that yield a mysterious glimmering beauty in the dark. Here is the "Zero at the Bone" of which Emily Dickinson, our supreme poet of inwardness, writes, with an urgency time has not blunted.

❄ ❄ ❄

My first immersion in the Literature of Despair came at a time of chronic adolescent insomnia, and so the ravishing experience of reading certain writers—most of them, apart from Dickinson and William Faulkner, associated with what was called European existentialism—is indelibly bound up with that era in my life. Perhaps the ideal reader *is* an adolescent: restless, vulnerable, passionate, hungry to learn, skeptical and naïve by turns; with an unquestioned faith in the power of the imagination to change, if not life, one's comprehension of life. To the degree to which we remain adolescents we remain ideal readers to whom the act of opening a book can be a sacred one, fraught with psychic risk. For each work of a certain magnitude means the assimilation of a new voice—that of Dostoyevsky's Underground Man, for instance, or Nietzsche's Zarathustra—and the permanent altering of one's own interior world.

Literary despair, as opposed to "real" despair, became fashionable at mid-century with a rich, diverse flood of English translations of European writers of surpassing originality, boldness, and genius. Misleadingly linked by so-called "Existentialist" themes, these highly individual writers—among them Dostoyevsky, Kafka, Kierkegaard, Mann, Sartre, Camus, Pavese, Pirandello, Beckett, Ionesco—seemed to characterize the very mission of literature itself: never in the service of "uplifting," still less "entertaining," but with a religious ideal of penetrating to the most inward and intransigent of truths. Despair at the randomness of mankind's fate and of mankind's repeatedly demonstrated inhumanity was in a sense celebrated, that we might transcend it through the symbolic strategies of art. For no fate, however horrific, as in the graphically detailed execution of the faithful officer of Kafka's great story "In the Penal Colony," or the ignominious execution of Joseph K. of Kafka's THE TRIAL—cannot be transmogrified by its very contemplation; or redeemed, in a sense, by the artist's visionary fearlessness. It is not just that despair is immune to the comforts of the ordinary—despair *rejects* comfort. And Kafka, our exemplary artist of despair, is one of our greatest humorists as well. The bleakness of his vision is qualified by a brash, unsettling humor that flies in the face of expectation. Is it tragic that Gregor Samsa is metamorphosed into a giant cockroach, suffers, dies, and is swept out with the trash?—is it tragic that the Hunger Artist starves to death, too finicky to eat the common food of humanity?—no, these are ludicrous fates, meant to provoke laughter. The self-loathing at the heart of despair repudiates compassion.

I would guess that my generation, coming of age at the very start of the Sixties and a national mood of intense political and moral crisis,

❧

is the last American generation to so contemplate *inwardness* as a romantic state of being; the last generation of literary-minded young men and women who interiorized the elegiac comedy of Beckett's characters, the radiant madness of Dostoyevsky's self-lacerated God-haunted seekers, the subtle ironies of Camus's prose. I doubt that contemporary adolescents can identify with Faulkner's Quentin Compson of THE SOUND AND THE FURY as, a Harvard freshman, he moves with the fatedness of a character in a ballad to his suicide by drowning in the Charles River—"People cannot do anything that dreadful they cannot do anything very dreadful at all they cannot even remember tomorrow what seemed dreadful today," Quentin's alcoholic father tells him, as if urging him to his doom. For even tragedy, in Faulkner's vision of a debased twentieth-century civilization, is "second-hand."

That this is a profound if dismaying truth, or an outrageous libel of the human spirit, either position to be confirmed by history, seems beside the point today, in a country in which politics has become the national religion. The Literature of Despair may posit suicide as a triumphant act of rebellion, or a repudiation of the meanness of life, but our contemporary mood is one of compassionate horror at any display of self-destruction. We perceive it, perhaps quite accurately, as misguided politics; a failure to link *in here* with *out there*.

For Americans, the collective belief, the moral imperative is an un-flagging optimism. We want to believe in the infinite elasticity of the future: what we *will*, we can *enact*. Just give us time—and sufficient resources. Our ethos has always been hardcore pragmatism as defined by our most eminent philosopher, William James: "truth" is something that happens to a proposition, "truth" is something that works. It is a vehicle empowered to carry us to our destination.

Yet there remains a persistent counterimpulse; an irresistible tug against the current; an affirmation of those awkward truths that, in Melville's words, will not be comforted. At the antipode of American exuberance and optimism there is the poet's small, still, private voice; the voice, most powerfully, of Emily Dickinson who, like Rilke, mined the ideal vocabulary for investigating those shifting, penumbral states of consciousness that do, in the long run, constitute our lives. Whatever our public identities may be, whatever our official titles, our heralded or derided achievements and the statistics that accrue to us like cob-webs, this is the voice we trust. For, if despair's temptations can be resisted, surely we become more human and compassionate; more like one another in our common predicament.

There is a pain—so utter—
It swallows substance up—
Then covers the Abyss with Trance—
So Memory can step
Around—across—upon it—
As one within a Swoon—
Goes safely—where an open eye—
Would drop Him—Bone by Bone.

—*Emily Dickinson*

The self's resilience in the face of despair constitutes its own transcendence. Even the possibility of suicide is a human comfort—a "carrion" comfort. In the Jesuit Gerard Manley Hopkins, extreme states of mind are confronted, dissected, overcome by the poet's shaping language:

I am gall, I am heartburn. God's most deep decree
Bitter would have me taste: my taste was me;
Bones built in me, flesh filled, blood brimmed the curse.

Selfyeast of spirit a dull dough sours. I see

The lost are like this, and their scourge to be

As I am mine, their sweating selves; but worse.

—"I Wake and Feel"

Not, I'll not, carrion comfort, Despair, not feast on thee;

Not untwist—slack they may be—these last strands of man

In me or, most weary, cry *I can no more.* I can;

Can something, hope, wish day come, not choose not to be.

But ah, but O thou terrible, why wouldst thou rude on me

Thy wring-earth right foot rock? lay a lionlimb against me?

   scan

With darksome devouring eyes my bruisèd bones? and fan,

O in turns of tempest, me heaped there; me frantic to avoid

   thee and flee?

—"Carrion Comfort"

These poems are among the most unsettling ever written; yet, in the way of all great art, they so passionately transcend their subject as to be a statement of humankind's strength, and not weakness.

THOMAS PYNCHON

Thomas Pynchon is the author of the novels V.; THE CRYING OF LOT 49; GRAVITY'S RAINBOW; VINELAND; and SLOW LEARNER, a collection of short stories. He was born and lives in the United States.

MARY GORDON

Mary Gordon is the author of four novels: FINAL PAYMENTS (1978); THE COMPANY OF WOMEN (1981); MEN AND ANGELS (1985); and THE OTHER SIDE (1989); as well as a short story collection, TEMPORARY SHELTER (1987); a collection of essays, GOOD BOYS AND DEAD GIRLS (1991); and three novellas, THE REST OF LIFE (1993). Born in Far Rockaway, New York, Ms. Gordon graduated from Barnard College and attended the writing program at Syracuse University. She currently resides in New York City with her husband and two children.

JOHN UPDIKE

John Updike has published some forty works including the famous RABBIT novels and, most recently, BRAZIL. He has won two Pulitzer Prizes for fiction and the National Book Critics Circle Award for criticism. A graduate of Harvard College in 1954, Mr. Updike went on to spend a year at the Ruskin School of Drawing and Fine Art in Oxford, England. From 1955 to 1957, he worked on the staff of THE NEW YORKER, to which he has contributed poems, short stories, essays, and book reviews. Born in Shillington, Pennsylvania, Mr. Updike currently lives in Massachusetts and has four children.

WILLIAM TREVOR

Born in County Cork, Ireland, in 1928, William Trevor graduated from Trinity College, Dublin, and went on to receive many coveted literary awards, including two Whitbread Prizes and The Royal Society of Literature Prize. His career has encompassed teaching and copywriting and to date he has over twenty books to his credit, including THE OLD BOYS (1964); THE DAY WE GOT DRUNK ON CAKE (1967); ANGELS AT THE RITZ (1973); and his latest, a collection of memoirs, EXCURSIONS IN THE REAL WORLD (1994). Mr. Trevor is also editor of THE OXFORD BOOK OF IRISH SHORT STORIES (1989).

❧

RICHARD HOWARD

Poet Richard Howard received a Pulitzer Prize in 1970 for UNTITLED SUBJECTS. He is author of ten books of poetry, including LIKE MOST REVELATIONS (1994), and of a critical study, ALONE WITH AMERICA (published in a second, enlarged edition in 1980). Poetry editor of THE PARIS REVIEW and Professor of English in the Creative Writing Program at the University of Houston, Mr. Howard is also a translator of some one hundred and fifty works from the French. He resides in New York City.

GORE VIDAL

Novelist, playwright, and critic, Gore Vidal published his first novel, WILLIAWAW, written in 1946 while in the army, and went on to write many others, including JULIAN (1964); MYRA BRECKINRIDGE (1968); and LIVE FROM GOLGOTHA (1992). He also is author of a multivolume chronicle of American history, starting with BURR (1973) and finishing with WASHINGTON, D.C. (1967), and of essays that have been collected in ROCKING THE BOAT (1962); REFLECTIONS ON A SINKING SHIP (1969); HOMAGE TO DANIEL SHAYS (1972); MATTERS OF FACT AND FICTION (1977); THE SECOND AMERICAN REVOLUTION (1982); and AT HOME (1988). His UNITED STATES: ESSAYS, 1952–1992 won the National Book Award for nonfiction. Mr. Vidal was born in 1925 at the United States Military Academy, West Point.

A. S. BYATT

Her novel POSSESSION earned A. S. Byatt both the coveted Booker Prize and IRISH TIMES/Aer Lingus International Prize in 1990. She is also author of several other works of fiction including THE SHADOW OF THE SUN; THE GAME; THE VIRGIN IN THE GARDEN; STILL LIFE; SUGAR AND OTHER STORIES; and ANGELS AND INSECTS. Ms. Byatt was educated in England at York and at Newnham College, Cambridge, and went on to teach at the Central School of Art before becoming a full-time writer. In 1990 she was appointed a C.B.E.

JOYCE CAROL OATES

Joyce Carol Oates is the author of twenty-three novels and of numerous story, poetry, and play collections. She has been the recipient of many prestigious prizes, including the National Book Award for THEM, the Rea Award for Achievement in the Short Story in 1990, and several O. Henry Awards for short fiction. Her 1990 novel BECAUSE IT IS BITTER AND BECAUSE IT IS MY HEART earned an NBA nomination and another, BLACK WATER, was nominated for a National Book Critics Circle Award. Ms. Oates resides in Princeton, New Jersey, where she is the Roger S. Berlind Distinguished Professor in the Humanities at Princeton University.

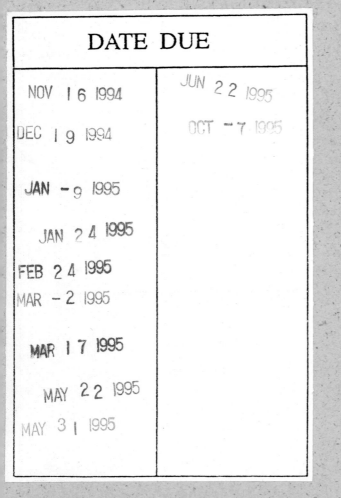